YOUR LAND AND MY LAND

We Visit
VENEZUELA

Doug Dillon

Mitchell Lane
PUBLISHERS
P.O. Box 196
Hockessin, Delaware 19707

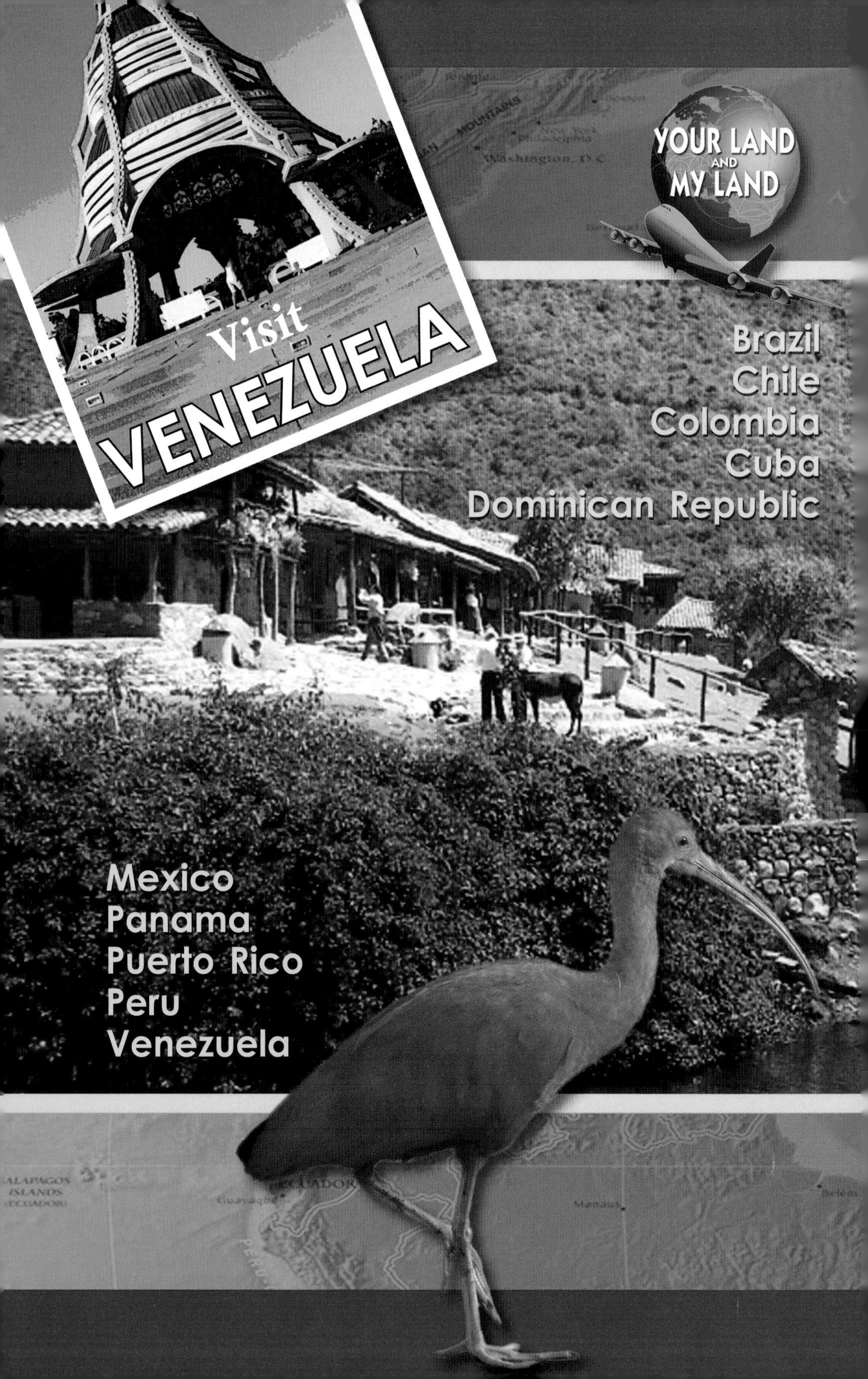

Visit
VENEZUELA

YOUR LAND
AND
MY LAND

Brazil
Chile
Colombia
Cuba
Dominican Republic

Mexico
Panama
Puerto Rico
Peru
Venezuela

YOUR LAND
AND
MY LAND

We Visit
VENEZUELA

Library of Congress Cataloging-in-Publication Data
Dillon, Douglas, 1943–
  We visit Venezuela / by Doug Dillon.
    p. cm. — (Your land and my land)
  Includes bibliographical references and index.
  ISBN 978-1-58415-884-4 (library bound)
  1. Venezuela—Juvenile literature. I. Title.
  F2308.5.D55 2011
  987—dc22
                                            2010026957

PUBLISHER'S NOTE: This story is based on the author's extensive research, which he believes to be accurate. Documentation of this research is on page 60.

The Internet sites referenced herein were active as of the publication date. Due to the fleeting nature of some web sites, we cannot guarantee they will all be active when you are reading this book.

To reflect current usage, we have chosen to use the secular era designations BCE ("before the common era") and CE ("of the common era") instead of the traditional designations BC ("before Christ") and AD (*anno Domini,* "in the year of the Lord").

PLB

Contents

Introduction 6

1 A Quick Peek 9

   Where in the World Is Venezuela? 12

   Facts at a Glance 13

2 Dipping into the Past.............................. 15

3 Who's in Charge?................................... 19

4 What's Venezuela Really Like?.............. 23

5 People and Everyday Living 29

6 Money and Business............................. 35

7 Up Close and Personal: Five Stories 39

8 Holidays and Celebrations 45

9 We Visit Venezuela 49

Venezuelan Recipe: Arepas 56

Venezuelan Craft: Devil Dancer Mask 57

Chapter Notes... 58

Timeline 60

Further Reading 60

   Books.. 60

   Works Consulted 60

   On the Internet 61

Glossary.. 62

Index 63

Introduction

Venezuela (veh-neh-ZWAY-lah) is part of a region called Latin America. This area of the world is south of the United States. It includes Mexico, Central America, South America, and the island countries that touch the Caribbean Sea, such as Haiti and the Dominican Republic. The U.S. Commonwealth of Puerto Rico is also part of Latin America.

Most people in Latin America speak Spanish, Portuguese (POR-choo-geez), or French. Those languages came from Latin—the language of the old Roman Empire—which is how Latin America got its name.

Venezuela is in northern South America, on the Caribbean Sea, and is a major gateway to South America for travelers from all over the world. This beautiful country with its natural wonders and friendly people gives visitors a taste of the many exciting things the surrounding continent has to offer.

The Regions and Countries of Latin America

Caribbean: Cuba, the Dominican Republic, French
    West Indies, Haiti, and Puerto Rico
North America: Mexico
Central America: Belize, Costa Rica, El Salvador,
    Guatemala, Honduras, Nicaragua, Panama
South America: Argentina, Bolivia, Brazil, Chile,
    Colombia, Ecuador, French Guiana, Guyana,
    Paraguay, Peru, Suriname, Uruguay,
    Venezuela

LATIN
AMERICA

Preparing for the Zaragoza Festival in Sanare, Lara, a man plays the cuatro, a Venezuelan four-stringed guitar. Music and festivals are important to the Venezuelan people.

A Quick Peek

Venezuela is a wild and wonderful mix of the old, the new, the beautiful, and the dangerous. While the country has a satellite in space and a large modern capital, it also has remote villages, old-time cowboys, and bullfights. It is a place where you can find some of the biggest shopping malls in South America as well as historic forts and churches.[1]

Venezuela sits at the top of South America. It is such a gorgeous place that when Christopher Columbus discovered it over 500 years ago, he thought he had found the Garden of Eden. A later visit by explorers from Spain named it Venezuela, which means "Little Venice." They called it that after they found Indians living over water in houses built on stilts. Those houses made the explorers think of Venice, an Italian city with waterways instead of pavement for streets.

If you flew over Venezuela, you would see a country with many different landforms. Parts of it are flat, other parts are mountainous, and in between are flat-topped mountains. Called *tepuis*, they look as if a giant has cut their tops off. There are lively beaches, scorching deserts, humid rain forests, misty cloud forests, thundering waterfalls, deep caves, a giant river system, and a great many islands.

In this Spanish-speaking country, the people are generally young and fun-loving. There are loads of things to do, from attending festivals and going shopping to mountain climbing and scuba diving. As people in the country would say, Venezuela is *chevre* (CHEH-veh-reh). When they say that, they mean something is very cool.[2]

The doorway into this country for most visitors is its capital, Caracas (kuh-RAH-kus). From Caracas you can fly just about anywhere in the country in about two hours. You can also drive along Venezuela's excellent network of well-maintained roads.

Caracas sits 3,000 feet (914 meters) high in a valley near the Caribbean Sea. The city's temperature stays close to a perfect 74°F (23°C). Between the Caribbean and Caracas are the tall mountains of Cordillera de la Costa, which include Ávila National Park.[3]

Caracas looks like any of the huge, modern cities of the world. With over 4 million people spread out over a large area, it has skyscrap-

Caracas, the capital of Venezuela, lies in a valley near the Caribbean Sea.

ers, superhighways, museums, and a subway system. Even so, many of its people live in poverty.[4] They live without electricity or running water in shacks set into the hills that surround the nicer parts of the capital. As in other large cities, crime and drug use are problems in Caracas.

FYI FACT:

The flat-topped mountains of Venezuela inspired Sir Arthur Conan Doyle to write a novel about them in 1912. He called it *The Lost World*— where dinosaurs live.

F1182 50¢

Sir Arthur Conan Doyle
THE LOST WORLD

A PROFESSOR CHALLENGER STORY

Where in the World

Caribbean Sea

Martinique (FR.)
Fort-de-France
SAINT LUCIA
Castries
SAINT VINCENT AND THE GRENADINES
Kingstown
Saint George's
GRENADA

Aruba (NETH.)
Oranjestad
Aruba
Netherlands Antilles (NETH.)
Curaçao
Willemstad
Bonaire

Caracas area states
1. YARACUY
2. CARABOBO
3. ARAGUA
4. MIRANDA

Puerto Bolívar
Golfo de Venezuela
Punto Fijo
Coro

Ríohacha
coal mine
FALCON
Riecito

Maracaibo
ZULIA
Cabimas
LARA
San Felipe
Puerto Cabello
Valencia
Maracay
Caracas
La Guaira
Los Teques
La Guaira

Tobago
Isla la Tortuga
NUEVA ESPARTA
Isla de Margarita
La Asunción
Port-of-Spain
TRINIDAD AND TOBA

DISTRITO FEDERAL

Cumaná
Barcelona
Güiria
Gulf of Paria
Trinidad

Maturín
SUCRE

Barquisimeto
Valera
TRUJILLO
Guanare
PORTUGUESA
San Carlos
COJEDES
San Juan de los Morros

Mérida
MÉRIDA
BARINAS
Barinas

Lago de Maracaibo

MONAGAS
Tucupita

Curiapo
D AMA

Cúcuta
San Cristóbal
TACHIRA
El Amparo
Arauca

Río Apure
APURE

San Fernando
Cabruta
Río Orinoco
Caicara

GUÁRICO
ANZOÁTEGUI

Ciudad Guayana
Ciudad Bolívar
dam
Guasipati
Bochinche

bucaramanga

Paz de Río
onja

San José del Guaviare
Calamar

Río Meta

El Jobal
iron mine

Ciudad Piar
Embalse de Guri
La Paragua

BOLÍVAR

Canaima

Río Caura
Río Caroni

El Dorado
Tumeremo

Puerto Carreño

Río Guaviare

Puerto Ayacucho

San Juan de Manapiare

Santa Elena de Uairén

COLOMBIA

San Fernando de Atabapo

Puerto Inírida

AMAZONAS

Esmeralda

Vila Brasil
No
B

Cucuí

Río Guainía

Río Casiquiare
Río Orinoco
Río Uraricoera

Boa Vista

Novo Paraíso

São Gabriel da Cachoeira

Río Branco

Río Negro

BRAZIL

Venezuela

———	International boundary
—·—·—	State-level boundary
★	National capital
⊙	State-level capital
+–+–+	Railroad
———	Road

0   50   100   150 Kilometers
0   50   100   150 Miles

Transverse Mercator Projection, CM 71° W

Bordering Colombia, Brazil, and Guyana, Venezuela also touches the Caribbean Sea and the Atlantic Ocean.

12

VENEZUELA FACTS AT A GLANCE

Venezuelan orchid

Official Country Name: Bolívarian Republic of Venezuela

Land Area: 340,561 square miles (882,050 square kilometers)

Size comparison: A little larger than twice the size of California

Highest Point: Pico Bolívar: 16,427 feet (5,007 meters)—just over 3 miles (5 kilometers)

Lowest Point: The Caribbean Sea (sea level)

Capital: Caracas

Other large cities: Mérida (MEH-ree-dah), Ciudad (thee-oo-DAHD), Bolívar (bo-LAY-var), Maracay (mah-rah-KAY), Valencia, Maracaibo (mar-uh-KY-boh), Barquisimeto (bar-kee-say-MAY-toh)

Population: 27,223,228 (July 2009 estimate)

Religions: Roman Catholic (96%), Protestant (2%), other (2%)

Literacy rate: 93%

Major product: Oil

Average temperature: 77°F (25°C)

Money: Bolívar Fuerte (foo-ERR-tey; the strong Bolívar); Symbol—Bs.F.

Form of Government: Federal Republic

Official language: Spanish

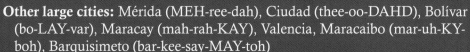

Flag: The flag has the country's coat of arms and three stripes: yellow for the wealth of Venezuela's land, blue for the courage of its people, and red for the blood shed to gain independence. Seven stars stand for the original seven states at the time of Venezuela's independence from Spain (President Hugo Chávez ordered the eighth star added in 2006).

National flower: Venezuelan orchid

National bird: Venezuelan troupial (*Icterus icterus*)

Source: *CIA World Factbook,* Venezuela

Many native peoples in Venezuela continue to practice traditional customs, including hunting and fishing.

Dipping into the Past

When Christopher Columbus arrived in Venezuela on August 1, 1498, he found people whose ancestors had lived there for thousands of years—including Carib, Arawak, and Chibcha peoples. It was his third voyage to that part of the world. The historical record shows that Columbus and his crew were almost certainly the first people from Europe to set foot on the continent of South America.

Columbus claimed all the land he saw and beyond for Spain. The Spaniards who arrived in Venezuela after him took over that land and made slaves of many indigenous people, whom they called Indians. The Spaniards were brutal, and their behavior sparked wars between them and the Indians.[1] As the Indians died from the wars and disease, the Spaniards brought in other slaves: people from Africa.

For over 300 years, Venezuela belonged to Spain. Because Venezuela did not have a lot of gold or silver, Spain paid little attention to it for a very long time. During those years, the big landowners in the country did pretty much what they wanted to do, without answering to the Spanish government.

When Spain started trying to control the landowners, they rebelled. By 1811, the War for Independence had begun.[2] After many years of fighting, an army under General Simón Bolívar (see-MOHN BOH-lee-var) defeated Spain, earning him the nickname El Libertador (The Liberator). By 1821, Bolívar and his army had kicked Spain out of large parts of South America that today are Colombia, Panama, and

Ecuador. Along with Venezuela, these countries became the Republic of Gran Colombia, with Bolívar as its president.

By 1830, Gran Colombia had fallen apart.[3] Venezuela then became a truly separate country with its own president, José (hoh-SAY) Antonio Páez (PAY-ez). In that same year, Bolívar died. Venezuela and other Latin American countries continue to remember him with great admiration for giving so many people their freedom from Spain. The country of Bolivia is named for him, and the money used in Venezuela bears his name—the Bolívar.

José Antonio Páez orders his cowboy followers to attack the Spanish cavalry in the War for Independence. Venezuelan artist Arturo Michelena painted this scene in the late 1800s.

In its early years as a country with its own leaders, Venezuela freed its slaves and had a terrible civil war, called the Federal War (1859–1863). Different groups fought to control the government. Strong rulers came and went, but in 1908, Juan Vicente Gómez (HWAN veh-SAHN-tay GOH-mez) became dictator of Venezuela. He ruled until 1935 with an iron hand, and he wasn't very popular.[4]

While Gómez was in power, a huge change swept through Venezuela. Oil was discovered in 1922, and Venezuela became a rich, oil-producing and -exporting nation. Oil experts and workers, especially from the United States, came to Venezuela to help develop this rich new resource.

FYI FACT:

When dictator Juan Vicente Gómez died in 1935, most people didn't believe the news. Since he hadn't always told the truth, they thought he was still alive and was trying to trick them.

The next big change came about in 1958, when Venezuela began electing its leaders. That year, Romulo Betancourt (RAH-moo-loh BEH-tahng-kort) became president. Since then, the people of the country have elected their presidents.[5] The country is officially a federal republic. Besides voting for the president, the citizens in Venezuela's 23 states also elect their state governments.

Venezuelan President Romulo Betancourt stands next to a statue of Simón Bolívar.

Hugo Chávez, president of Venezuela, intro-
duced a new constitution in 1999, then revised
it several times during his presidency.

Chapter 3

Who's in Charge?

The people of Venezuela have a long history of being unhappy with their government. That dissatisfaction became even stronger in the last part of the twentieth century. When oil prices dropped, the country had less money, and its many poor people grew even poorer. Crime and violence in the cities increased at the same time.

By 1992, young army officers, including Hugo Chávez, decided to change things by taking over the government by force. This attempt failed. Chávez and the other officers were arrested.[1] After his release from jail, Chávez joined the MVR political party. In 1998, he ran for president mainly against female candidate Irene Sáez. Supported mostly by the country's poor, Chávez won and took office in 1999.

Chávez has made many changes in his country—some of them popular and others not. Many of these changes, he said, were to help the poor. One of the first things he did was to honor Simón Bolívar. He changed the name of the country to the Bolívarian Republic of Venezuela. He also called people together to write a new constitution. Late in 1999, this new constitution became the law of the land, with some changes made later, in 2004.

Venezuela's constitution provides for a president who serves for six years but can be reelected. A group of 167 people elected to the National Assembly creates the country's laws. The highest court in the land, the Supreme Tribunal of Justice, consists of thirty-two judges. The five-member National Electoral Council organizes national elections.

Citizen Power, with three people running it, is the final part of the government. One person, the comptroller, keeps track of the country's finances. Another person, called the ombudsman, investigates complaints people make against schools or businesses and helps them solve those problems. The third person is the Attorney General, who brings people or companies to court for violating laws.[2]

There are many political parties in Venezuela. Some of them are The United Socialist Party (PSUV), Democratic Action (AD), The Christian Democrats (COPEI), Fatherland For All (PPT), and Movement Toward Socialism (MAS). President Hugo Chávez represents the Fifth Republic Movement (MVR). The initials listed after each of these names stand for the name of each party in Spanish.[3]

To bring about other changes, Chávez started increasing the control of government over business and the economy. So many people opposed those changes that in 2002, hundreds of thousands marched against him in downtown Caracas. They demanded that he resign as president. When he did not, the military moved in and arrested him.[4]

During 2002, hundreds of thousands of people protested against the government of Hugo Chávez in Caracas.

Under a painting of Simón Bolívar, Venezuelan President Hugo Chávez (right) and Colombian President Alvaro Uribe met at Miraflores Palace for a press conference on Feburary 15, 2005. This was the first meeting to discuss problems between their two countries.

Soon after, another group in the military freed him, and again he was president. Since that time, Chávez has been reelected as president and he has increased his control over life in Venezuela. He calls his actions the "Bolívarian Revolution." In 2009, the people of Venezuela voted to allow Chávez to run for president as many times as he wants.[5] Up until then, the constitution limited Chávez to two terms in office at six years each.

For divers, Los Roques chain of islands offers warm, transparent water and a tremendous variety of sea life. Part of a large barrier reef, Los Roques is one of the most undamaged of such reefs in the Caribbean Sea.

What's Venezuela Really Like?

Venezuela is the sixth largest country in South America. Colombia, Brazil, and Guyana are the three nations that share its borders. Venezuela is also the home of the Orinoco (or-uh-NOH-koh) River System, one of the largest on the continent.

The northern part of Venezuela has a long and beautiful coastal region. It stretches east and west for over 1,700 miles (2,740 kilometers) along the Caribbean Sea, even reaching the Atlantic Ocean. There, clear blue-green water meets mostly white sand beaches, palm trees, and even dense rain forest growth.

Just off its coast, Venezuela governs many islands, including Margarita Island and the archipelago of Los Roques (The Rocks). Tourists love both places, mainly because of the great beaches there, as well as excellent scuba diving and snorkeling opportunities. Besides Gran Roque, on which there is a large town, the archipelago of Los Roques has over 300 small islands. Made of mostly coral reefs, many of them go under water at high tide.[1]

The island country of Trinidad and Tobago nearly touches the northeast coast of Venezuela. It is in this area that the Orinoco and other rivers dump their freshwater into the Atlantic Ocean. This huge flow of water brings dirt with it and creates a giant triangle of mud called a delta. Few people live in this wild and watery area, but mangrove trees, red howler monkeys, giant otters, and anacondas do.

Most cities in this country are located in a region called the Venezuelan Highlands. This area starts out as a series of low mountains along

Although part of Venezuela, Los Roques lies 80 miles (120 kilometers) north of the port of Guaira in Caracas. Numbering more than 300 and covering an area of over 40 square miles (104 square kilometers), these islands attract many visitors, especially from Europe.

the Caribbean coast. It then connects in the west with an arm of the Andes, the longest mountain chain in the world. The capital, Caracas, sits in a valley of these highlands.

In the northwest part of Venezuela lies an area called the Maracaibo Lowlands. It is lowland because all the land there sweeps downward from the mountains on three sides to Lake Maracaibo. This giant body of water, the largest natural lake in South America, empties into the Caribbean Sea. In its waters, mullet swim and pink flamingos wade, but beneath the muddy lakebed sits much of the oil that makes Venezuela wealthy.[2]

Central Venezuela is mostly very flat and has only little groups of trees near its rivers. Called Los Llanos (LOHS YAH-nohs), or The Plains (flatlands), it is home to giant anteaters and the troupial, Venezuela's national bird. Los Llanos makes up one third of Venezuela's land area, about equal to the size of Italy.[3]

Millions of cattle also roam Los Llanos, and they outnumber the people who live there. The cowboys who take care of them are called *llaneros* (yah-NAYR-rohs). Venezuelans greatly respect their cowboys, and very much enjoy the songs they sing.

South and east of the Orinoco are the Guiana Highlands, which take up about half the country. This is a land of many rivers, dense tropical forests, and high, flat-topped mountains. The local Pemón Indians named these mountains *tepuis* (tey-POO-ees). In their language, the word means "Houses of the Gods." The tallest of these *tepuis*, Mount Roraima (roo-RY-mah), is slightly over 9,200 feet (2,800 meters) high.[4] Huge waterfalls crash from near the top of many *tepuis*.

Venezuela's tallest flat-topped mountain, or *tepui*, is Mount Roraima. Also known as Tepui Roraima, it borders the countries of Brazil and Guyana.

With so many highlands and mountains, Venezuela has many giant caves. The largest, Cave of the Guácharo (GWAH-chah-roh, which means "oilbirds"), has 6 miles (10 kilometers) of passageways. It was named for the thousands of oilbirds that live in it. These nocturnal birds feed on the fruit of oil palms. Another, Cave of the Ghost, has an opening so big that two helicopters could fly through right next to each other.[5] Some caves are actually huge sinkholes that go straight down over 300 feet (100 meters).

Certain parts of Venezuela get so little rain that they have become deserts. One such place is in the state of Falcón (fol-KON) on the Caribbean coast. Sticking out into that sea is a little bubble of land with huge sand dunes and plenty of cacti. This is the Paraguaná (par-uh-gwan-NAH) Peninsula north of the city of Coro. Tourists visiting

The oilbird, also known as the *guácharo*, is a slim, long-winged bird found in the northern areas of South America. This night-flying species feeds on the oil palm and tropical laurels. It can hover and twist in flight, which allows it to fly easily through tight spaces inside caves.

that area can ride camels across the sand dunes, just as people do in the Sahara.

Since it is located just above the equator, Venezuela is a tropical country. This means it has a mostly hot and humid climate. The temperature averages 77°F (25°C), and there are only two seasons, wet and dry. The wet season is May through November. In Los Llanos, the wet season brings floods. The dry season lasts from around December through April.

The climate varies the most, however, in the highlands and mountain regions. As elevation increases, the temperature drops. In the highest Venezuelan Andes, it is as cold as winter in Alaska all year.

The rain forests, cloud forests, deserts, highlands, and mountain areas in this country contain a great variety of plant species. Scientists continue to discover new ones. From orchids to cacti, Venezuela has plants that live in a wide range of climates.

Living in this country's waters and on its land are thousands of species of creatures. Parrots, toucans, macaws, and capuchin monkeys glide through the treetops in the rain forest. Eagles and condors nest on ledges of tall mountains and *tepuis*, and flesh-eating piranhas lurk in rivers and streams. Reptiles such as caimans, the Orinoco crocodile, and the green anaconda hunt capybaras, the largest rodents in the world, near the river's edge. Huge swordfish and tarpon patrol Venezuela's coastline, while pumas and jaguars roam the country's tropical grasslands.

FYI FACT:

The green anacondas of Venezuela are among the largest snakes in the world. They can grow up to 30 feet (9 meters) long and weigh up to 550 pounds (227 kilograms).[6]

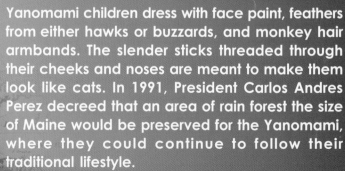

Yanomami children dress with face paint, feathers from either hawks or buzzards, and monkey hair armbands. The slender sticks threaded through their cheeks and noses are meant to make them look like cats. In 1991, President Carlos Andres Perez decreed that an area of rain forest the size of Maine would be preserved for the Yanomami, where they could continue to follow their traditional lifestyle.

Chapter 5

People and Everyday Living

Young is a key word when thinking about the people of Venezuela. Half the country's 27 million–plus population is under twenty-five years old.[1] Perhaps that's one reason why nearly everyone in Venezuela always seems ready to have a good time.

Most people live in the cities, but a great many of them are very poor no matter where their homes are located. Other citizens—those with good jobs and money—support many modern shopping malls. One example is the Centro Sambil Mall in Caracas, the fourth largest in all of South America. It has five levels, amusement rides, theaters, restaurants, and more than 500 stores.[2] Like U.S. malls, shops there and in other cities offer buyers just about anything they could want.

Venezuela's indigenous people, or Indians, now make up only 2 percent of the country's population. They generally keep to themselves, away from population centers, but some do live in cities such as Maracaibo. Others frequent the cities only to sell products they make, such as hammocks, and to buy things they need.

There are two major Indian groups in Venezuela. South of the Orinoco River, and mostly in the state of Amazonas, live the Yanomami (yah-noh-MAH-mee). These are deep-jungle people who live much as they did 8,000 years ago.[3] Their villages are small, with houses made from forest materials. Each house contains more than one family. Yanomami tend small garden plots and hunt using blowguns. They dip their darts in the deadly slime of poison dart frogs.[4]

In the Lake Maracaibo region live the Guajiros (gwah-HEE-rohs). A nomadic people, they move back and forth across the border of Venezuela and Colombia. Some have settled in Maracaibo and smaller towns, where there is more work than in the dry regions, coastal areas, and forests where most of them live.

Along the coast and in Caracas live many of the people who can trace their history back to the Africans who were brought into the country as slaves hundreds of years ago. Those enslaved Africans worked plantations for white people under terrible conditions. Their descendents make up about 5 percent of the population.

Over the years, other groups of people have come to live in Venezuela. Most of them arrived from Europe—from Spain, Italy, Germany, and Portugal. About 10 percent of Venezuela's population can say they have a pure European background. Others are Arabs from the Middle East and people from Asia. Today, however, at least 67 percent of Venezuelans have a mixed-race background, with some combination of European (mostly Spanish), Indian, and African.[5]

Besides Spanish, many people speak English. There is also a wide variety of other languages spoken by the country's many Indian groups.

Most Venezuelans—96 percent—are Roman Catholic.[6] The practice of this religion combines many cultures. The Virgin Mary and the Catholic saints are important to many Venezuelans. People pray to them, and even small towns have one saint who they believe is their patron, or protector. During festivals, they parade statues of these saints and the Virgin Mary through the streets. Along with the beliefs brought to this country from Spain are traces of African Voodoo and Indian religions. This blending of magic and legends from traditions other than European has made Venezuela's version of the Catholic religion a rich and fascinating spiritual mixture.[7]

Families are truly at the heart of Venezuelan society. In this country, "family" includes all the aunts, uncles, cousins, and grandparents, as well as parents and children. Everyone is usually extremely close. They often visit each other, eat meals together, and have big parties. Weddings, baptisms, and funerals are important religious events that all family members usually attend.[8]

If families are at the heart of Venezuelan society, then women are its soul. It is the women—the mothers, grandmothers, and aunts—who truly keep everyone together and make things happen. Officially, however, it is the men—the fathers, grandfathers, and uncles—who make most of the big family decisions.[9]

Young people in Venezuela have to attend school at least through tenth grade and age fifteen. There are private schools that charge money, but the public schools are free. Basic public school education goes up to twelfth grade. Venezuela's Ministry of Education controls the schools, and it spends 7 percent of all the wealth produced in Venezuela. About 93 percent of the people can read.

After twelfth grade, students have many educational options. There are 24 private universities and 23 public universities, as well as 74 other types of schools of higher learning. Discoveries made by scientists from these schools add greatly to the world's knowledge. In 2003, for example, Antonio Machado from Venezuela's Central University

Preparing for the future, students in a Caracas math class compete with each other to show their teacher they know the answer.

directed a project that found ten new species of fish in Venezuela. One of those fish turned out to be a piranha that enjoys eating fruit as well as flesh. Nine percent of the country's workers have attended college.[10]

The unique blend of Indian, African, and European cultures is evident all across Venezuela—in the music, foods, and festivals. Cultural influences from the United States also continue to shape the nation. Venezuela has professional sports such as basketball, horseracing, bullfighting, and boxing. The most loved sport, however, is baseball. Oil workers from the United States brought this sport to Venezuela in the early twentieth century, and now kids all over the country play it. Many Venezuelans also enjoy watching U.S. movies and television programs. *The Simpsons* and *Baywatch Hawaii* are two U.S. programs seen on Venezuelan TV.

Many people in Venezuela watch telenovelas. These are TV shows much like U.S. soap operas. The programs are about complicated romances between adults who must sort through the problems of life. Most telenovelas are produced in Mexico, Colombia, and Brazil, but they are popular all over Latin America. Spanish-speaking people in the United States, Canada, and other parts of the world watch them as well.

In Venezuela, a person's appearance is very important. Most people take great pride in being as neat, nicely dressed, and attractive as possible. This is especially true for women. People there look down upon others who are the least bit sloppy, even visiting tourists. For example, many museums and religious buildings have dress codes: some won't let anybody in who is wearing shorts, for example.[11]

In most countries, beauty contests are not as popular as they once were, but they remain an important business in Venezuela. Every year, people all over the country follow the Miss Venezuela Contest. Pageant winners go on to compete in either the Miss World or the Miss Universe contest. Venezuela has produced more international beauty queens than any other country.

Newspapers, as well as radio and TV stations, follow these contests closely. While the lives of the young women who compete become fodder for gossip, the experience and celebrity status of these women help them find meaningful jobs later on.[12]

When the weather gets hot, city people (and tourists) head for the beaches or the cool mountains. They hike through national parks, or go rock climbing, caving, paragliding, river rafting, canoeing, or skiing. Right outside Caracas is a park in the mountains—Ávila (AH-vee-yah) National Park. Along Venezuela's coastal regions, visitors can bask in the sun and have their pick of water sports.

Fun time in Venezuela also involves music and dance. During festivals, there is even dancing in the streets. Everybody is expected to take part. Salsa is one favorite. The country's national dance, *joropo* (hoh-ROH-poh), is another.

Many native tribes continue to play traditional types of music. Often, it has to do with spirits and healing. They mainly use flutes, drums, and other percussion instruments.[13] In the coastal areas of the country, much of the music is drumming of all kinds. Clearly heard in these drums is the influence of Africa.

Most music in Venezuela traces its roots back to Spain. Much of it uses the guitar and harp and comes from Los Llanos—cowboy country. Over the years, people in Los Llanos have created their own four-stringed guitar called the cuatro (KWAH-troh).

The capital of Caracas has five major orchestras. Each state capital has its own orchestra as well. In the field of dance, Venezuela has several well-known ballet companies. One of the most famous is the National Ballet of Caracas.

Venezuela's national dish is *pabellón criollo* (pay-bel-YOHN KREE-yoh). It is a combination of shredded beef, white rice, black beans, grated cheese, and fried plantains (banana-like tropical fruits). The most common food is the arepa (ah-RAY-pah). This is toasted white cornbread that can be eaten plain or filled with cheese, shredded beef or chicken, black beans, chopped eggs, tomatoes, onions, or avocados.

Some favorite drinks are coffee, rum, tropical fruit juices, and coconut milk. These are made from plants that are farmed in the country. Even the rum comes from Venezuelan sugar.

A Petroleums of Venezuela, SA, processing plant in Puerto La Cruz. Known by its Spanish initials of PDVSA, this huge oil and natural gas company helps make Venezuela the fifth largest oil exporter in the world.

Chapter

6

Money and Business

Venezuela has one of the strongest economies in all of Latin America. In 2008, it produced $315.6 billion in wealth.[1] However, the government controls much of the country's money. It spends over 30 percent of it every year.

Twenty-eight percent of Venezuela's wealth comes from the pumping, processing, and sale of oil. This creates many jobs and inexpensive gasoline for its people. But the government keeps very tight control of this industry. Half the money the government takes in comes from oil.[2]

For a long time, oil kept Venezuela's economy going strong. The wealth it produced also helped to improve the country. The government was able to build roads, schools, and hospitals.

Over time, a major problem arose. When the price of oil went way down in the 1980s, there wasn't enough money to maintain the level of wealth or the number of jobs. This close tie between the economy and the oil industry continues to be a problem as the price of oil changes.

Hydroelectric power supplies much of this country's energy needs. Energy produced by the Guri (goo-REE) Dam on the Caroni (kah-ROH-nee) River supplies about 70 percent of Venezuela's electricity. Without the dam, the country would have to burn a lot more oil to create power. The government estimates that using hydroelectric power saves 300,000 barrels of oil each year.

The country has other important natural resources—such as iron ore, bauxite, zinc, natural gas, coal, diamonds, and gold—that also

Construction for Venezuela's Guri Dam in Bolívar State on the Caroni River began in 1963 and ended in 1986. As of 2010, this hydroelectric plant—at 4,265 feet long (1,300 meters) and 531 feet high (162 meters)—was the third largest in the world.

provide wealth and jobs.[3] Venezuela's government believes its country has 12 percent of the world's gold that no one has dug up yet.

Bauxite is an ore mined from the ground and used to make aluminum. Until it found its own bauxite in 1977, Venezuela had to buy it from other countries. After that, its aluminum industry grew rapidly. Now it exports both aluminum and bauxite. It also exports a lot of its iron ore and steel, which is made by mixing iron with carbon.

In factories, Venezuela makes paper products, textiles (fabrics and their products), plastics, cement, and transportation equipment, including cars. Some of these cars are exported.[4]

FYI FACT:

Long ago, the sale of cacao plant seeds, which are used to make chocolate, helped to build Venezuela. In the 1700s, people in Europe bought great quantities of Venezuelan cacao seeds because they loved chocolate-flavored drinks.

Although less than 5 percent of the land supports farming, and it produces only about 4.6 percent of Venezuela's wealth, more people work in this area than in the oil industry. Some of the major crops are corn, sorghum, rice, coffee, cacao, bananas, cotton, vegetables, and sugarcane. However, there aren't enough farms and farm workers to grow enough food, so Venezuela has to import a lot of it from other countries.[5]

Ranches use about 20 percent of the land and raise a great deal of beef cattle. Other key agricultural products are pork, milk, eggs, and fish.

A few of the seaports for trading with other countries are La Guaira (GWAH-ee-rah), Maracaibo, and Puerto Cabello (kah-BAY-yoh). Close to $70 billion in exports and $46 billion in imports pass through the ports of Venezuela each year.[6]

Even though Venezuela is considered a wealthy country, it still has a lot of money problems. For a very long time, this country's money has been losing value. By 2009, the inflation rate was close to 30 percent per year. That means a product that cost 3 Bolívars Fuerte in 2008 cost almost 4 Bolívars Fuerte in 2009.

In 2008, President Hugo Chávez changed the money to help make it more valuable. He also made it more colorful and gave it a new name. The old money was the Bolívar; the new is the Bolívar Fuerte. In Spanish, that means "strong Bolívar." Some people think the name change is just wishful thinking. In Venezuela, the symbol for Bolívars Fuerte is Bs. F.

Caracas-born Francisco Rodriguez pitches for the New York Mets. In 2008, Rodriguez held the major-league record with 62 saves in a single season.

Chapter

7

Up Close and Personal: Five Stories

Venezuelans have become famous in many fields, from entertainment to politics. Here are the stories of four Venezuelans: a baseball player, Francisco Rodriguez; a beauty queen turned politician, Irene Sáez; an entertainer, Simón Díaz; and a writer, Teresa de la Parra. Jimmie Angel, an American pilot, became famous for introducing Angel Falls to the world.

Francisco Rodriguez
His friends call him Frankie. Fans call him K-Rod—short for "Kid Rodriguez." He is one of Venezuela's best young pitchers to play professional baseball in the United States.

Born in Caracas in 1982, Francisco Rodriguez went to live with his grandparents after his parents divorced. His new neighborhood was very poor, but somehow his grandmother managed to get him into a baseball school. That is where he learned how to throw his famous fastball.

By age twenty, he was in the United States and playing for the Anaheim Angels. In 2002, he helped them win the World Series. In 2008, the New York Mets signed him up for three years starting in 2009. The value of that contract was $37 million.[1]

As famous as he is, Rodriguez still goes back to his old baseball school in Venezuela. There he talks to the kids and teaches them how to play the game.

Irene Sáez

The best known of all of Venezuela's beauty queens is Irene Sáez. In 1981 at the age of twenty, she won the Miss Venezuela pageant. Later, she went on to take the Miss Universe crown in New York City.

Smart as well as beautiful, Irene then went to college and earned a degree in political science. After graduation, a bank hired her to appear in its TV ads. This made her even more popular than she had been as a beauty queen. Venezuela sent her to the United Nations in New York City to represent her country's culture.

In 1992, Sáez entered politics—mostly a man's world in Venezuela. She ran for mayor of Chacao (chah-KAW), a part of Caracas. She won that election and did such a good job she was reelected in 1995.[2]

By 1998, so many people knew about and liked this former beauty queen that she ran for president. Sáez campaigned hard, but the people of Venezuela elected Hugo Chávez for the first time instead.

Three months later, Sáez ran for governor of Nueva Sparta, a state in Venezuela. That time she won with more than 70 percent of the vote.[3]

Simón Díaz

One of the most important names in Venezuelan music is Simón Díaz. Born in Los Llanos, Díaz made the music of that area famous. In over 70 albums, he has preserved the music of the *llaneros*. He writes and sings his own songs, which have been translated into ten different languages. One of them became a worldwide hit. Called "Caballo Viejo" (kah-BAH-yo vee-AH-oh, meaning "Old Horse"), it tells the story of a man who falls in love with a girl that people say is too young for him. Many different singers and singing groups have recorded

that song, as well as others Díaz wrote.[4]

Not just a singer and songwriter, Díaz is also an actor, radio star, TV star, TV producer, and comedian. For ten years, he hosted a children's television program. During that time, he taught his audience about Venezuelan culture. They knew him as "Uncle Simón."

To recognize his importance to the country's culture, Venezuela gave Díaz its highest award—the Liberator's Order. Two Venezuelan universities gave him honorary degrees, and in 2008, he received an honorary Latin Grammy music award.

Teresa de la Parra

Born of rich parents in 1889, Teresa de la Parra became a famous writer in Venezuela. She started out writing articles for newspapers, then began crafting fiction.

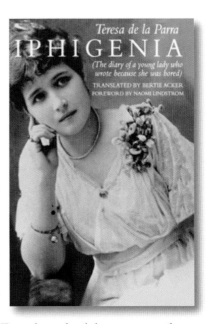

In 1924, she published her first novel in Paris, called *Iphigenia (The Diary of a Young Lady Who Wrote Because She Was Bored)*. De la Parra's female character in this story rebels against the traditional expectations that people have of women in Venezuela. The book became very popular, but many men in Venezuela spoke out against it.[5]

Iphigenia made De la Parra famous. People asked her to speak at colleges and conferences. She completed her second novel, *Souvenirs*

After pilot Jimmie Angel discovered this huge waterfall flowing from near the top of Auyantepui in Venezuela's Bolívar State, the Venezuelan government named the place Angel Falls in his honor.

of *Mama Blanca,* in 1929. Soon after that, she began working on a novel about the life of Simón Bolívar.

In 1932, De la Parra got very ill with tuberculosis. In those days, the disease was quite deadly. After a long stay in a hospital, and still very sick, De la Parra decided to visit Spain. Her doctor tried to change her mind but she went anyway. In 1936, she died in Spain without being able to finish her novel about Bolívar.[6]

Jimmie Angel

In 1933, American pilot Jimmie Angel was looking for a *tepui* in the Venezuelan Highlands that was supposed to have a river of gold. He didn't find it, but he did fly over a very tall *tepui* with a giant waterfall. Angel figured the waterfall had to be a mile long. When he returned from his flight, nobody believed him about the tall mountain or the waterfall.

In 1937, Angel was able to find the same *tepui* and waterfall once more. He tried landing on the mountain's flat top but wrecked his airplane. On board were his wife and two friends (Gustavo Heny and Miguel Angel Delgado). No one was injured, but it took them eleven days of climbing and hacking through the rain forest to find help. Angel did not find any gold, but people finally believed him about the waterfall.

For thirty years, Angel's plane rested on top of the *tepui.* Eventually, the Venezuelan Air Force brought it down piece by piece. Today, it sits in front of the passenger terminal at the airport outside Bolívar City.[7]

Jimmie Angel died in 1956, but the water-fall he discovered bears his name—Angel Falls. At 3,212 feet (979 meters) high—nearly six-tenths of a mile—it is about twenty times taller than Niagara Falls.

A Caracas Independence Day parade celebrates Venezuela's separation from Spain.

Chapter 8

Holidays and Celebrations

Holidays in Venezuela often have to do with religion, with the calendar of the Roman Catholic Church setting the stage for many major celebrations. These are fun times as well as spiritual. People get together to eat and drink, wear costumes, have colorful parades, play music, and dance.[1] Many also go to the beach or to the mountains.

In parades, people carry religious figures that are important in different regions of the country. Some regions have additional special holidays as well. Some people in Venezuela also celebrate the U.S. holidays of Thanksgiving and Valentine's Day.

National Public Holidays[2]
January 1—New Year's Day
February or March (2 days)—Carnival (kar-nih-VAL)
March or April—Holy Week, with Holy Thursday the focal point of the entire week's celebration
April 19—Declaration of Independence Day (from Spain)
May 1—Labor Day
June 24—Battle of Carabobo (kah-rah-BO-bo) (An important victory over Spain by Simón Bolívar)
July 5—Independence Day (Actual separation from Spain)
July 24—Simón Bolívar's Birthday
October 12—Day of Indigenous Resistance (fighting against the Spanish)
December 25—Christmas Day

Day of the Innocents

On December 28 in some parts of Venezuela, people remember a devastating event that took place soon after the birth of Jesus. As recorded in the Bible, King Herod killed all the male babies in his kingdom, hoping Jesus would be one of them.

On this day each year in Venezuela, children dress up in costumes and play jokes on people to make up for the sadness. The adults dress up as well. To the sounds of music, they dance and parade around the streets with the children.[3]

Carnival

Carnival (or *Carnaval* in Spanish) lasts from Saturday through Tuesday and falls in either February or March, just before the Catholic observance of Lent. Lent—the 40 days before Easter—is when many Catholics give up something that gives them pleasure, such as eating chocolate or drinking soda.[4] Carnival is the last chance they get to enjoy those things before Lent.

Originally celebrated in Spain, Carnival is an important holiday in many parts of Latin America. Many people in Caracas and other big cities simply leave for the beach or the mountains. But in the smaller towns and cities, there are huge parades. People wear elaborate costumes, and some dress up as crazy devils. This kind of celebrating is

Girls in costumes at a carnival in Güigüe, Venezuela

a lot like what happens throughout Latin America and at Mardi Gras in New Orleans, Louisiana.

Holy Week

The week before the Christian celebration of Easter is Holy Week, with most of the celebrations happening on Thursday. Held in either March or April, it is a mixture of religious observances and celebrations. Some people go away for this holiday. Others parade in the street. Some act out the Bible story of Easter—how Jesus died on the cross and what happened afterward.[5]

Dancing Devils of Yare

Every year in either May or June, on the Roman Catholic Feast Day of Corpus Christi,[6] devils dance in the small town of San Francisco de Yare near Caracas. Tourists come from all over the world to see this event.

Devil dancing began in Spain centuries ago. Then Africans along the coast of Venezuela adopted the practice in the late 1700s. This was a way for them to play an important part in Venezuela's Catholic religion.[7]

Men dress in red and yellow and wear huge, horrible devil masks. They parade and dance through the streets of Yare for many hours, pretending to scare people and to bring evil to the town. Finally, the dancers stop in front of a church. There they have a ceremony and bow before God. Good has won over evil.

The Metropolitan Cathedral of Mérida took 150 years to build. Begun in the early 1800s, two major earthquakes and Venezuela's War for Independence interrupted its construction.

We Visit Venezuela

Most tourists who want to explore Venezuela start in the bustling city of Caracas. There are world-class art museums, including the modern Museo de Arte Contemporaneo, and centuries-old churches. Simón Bolívar's family worshiped in Catedral Metropolitana de Caracas, built at the end of the 1600s. Its spectacular altar is gilded with over 300 pounds of gold. His birthplace and a museum to honor him, Casa Natal & Museo Bolívar, are also in Caracas. Another church that is popular with tourists is Iglesia de San Francisco, where Bolívar's massive funeral was held in 1830. In the old section of town stands the National Pantheon of Venezuela, where Bolívar and other national heroes are buried. Murals depicting scenes of Bolívar's life adorn the walls.

Other places to visit are the Federal Palace and the Legislative Palace, where the National Assembly meets. These buildings were completed in 1873 and 1877, respectively. The Museo de Ciencias Naturales is a natural history museum that features exhibits on the early indigenous people of Venezuela.

Monuments abound, including the striking Arco de la Federación, which was built in 1895 in remembrance of the Federal War. One of the oldest parks in the city, Parque Los Caobos, features a fountain with bronze sculptures that is over 100 years old.

For tourists who want to see the variety of wildlife that Venezuela has to offer, el Teleférico (the cable car) takes passengers from Caracas high into the mountains. It will drop them off at 7,000 feet (2,135 meters) above sea level in Ávila National Park, or carry them down the other side of the mountain to the city of Macuto.

Angel Falls

One of the most awesome sights in the world is Angel Falls (see page 42). Its water thunders down from two openings in the side of Auyantepui (ay-YAN-teh-POO-ee), one of Venezuela's billion-year-old, flat-topped mountains. Those two huge, gushing streams then merge far below. When seen from a distance, they make a big V.[1]

Averaging only about 350 feet (110 meters) wide, it is the tallest waterfall in the world. It starts out about 50 feet (15 meters) from the top of Auyantepui and falls nearly 2,700 feet (825 meters) before it hits rock.[2]

Once it smashes into the rocks, the water drops for another 500 feet (150 meters). Before hitting the ground, however, most of it turns to mist, and it breaks into several much smaller waterfalls. At the bottom is a pool of cool water where visitors can swim.

This beautiful place is located in the middle of Venezuela's Guiana Highlands and is part of Canaima (kah-NY-mah) National Park. Surrounded by rain forest and other *tepuis,* the only ways to get there are by airplane or boat.

The local Pemón (PAY-mon) Indians act as guides for tourists and transport them to the falls in canoes. The ancestors of these Indians discovered the falls long before Jimmie Angel flew over the area. They call the falls Kerepakupai Merú—Waterfall of the Deepest Place.[3]

The Orinoco Delta

The Orinoco Delta region, found right along the coast of northeast Venezuela, is so large that most of it creates one of this country's states, Delta Amacuro (ah-mah-KOO-roh).[4] This triangular area is a maze of practically countless islands.

On the delta are rain forests and acres of mangrove swamps. Travel is by swift motorboat or even dugout canoe in the many waterways. In this habitat lurk jaguars, giant river otters, anacondas, and river dolphins. In the early morning, screams of howler monkeys scare huge flocks of colorful birds into the air. In the tangle of plants on both

Stilt houses allow Warao Indians to live directly above the water in the wild Orinoco Delta region of Venezuela's Delta Amacuro State.

sides of these waterways, scarlet ibis and gold macaws flash their brilliant colors. Guided by the local Warao (wah-RAH-oh) Indians, tourists can fish for piranhas.

Tourists are welcome to visit Warao Indian villages built on stilts over the water. If you are lucky, the Warao might even offer you one of their favorite foods—grub worms.[5] Try them raw, boiled, or fried.

Margarita Island

One of Venezuela's most popular vacation spots is Margarita Island, which sits just off the country's Caribbean coast. Known all over the world, the island offers dazzling beaches and quiet little fishing villages.[6] Tourists arrive by airplane or ferry.

This curved vacation spot is one of Margarita Island's many beaches. Venezuelans and foreign tourists come to this Caribbean island mostly to enjoy its water sports.

Margarita Island is actually two pieces of land connected by a thin strip of desert-like sand. The western half is hot and dry and does not have many trees or people. In the eastern half, the climate is much more pleasant, with lots of trees, gorgeous sandy coastline, and modern hotels.

Most people go to Margarita Island to swim, fish, snorkel, scuba dive, drive personal water scooters, surf, and windsurf. Others like to shop, go horseback riding, visit some of the many historic churches, or walk through a centuries-old fort. There are also caves to explore and rocks to climb.

If you like museums, don't miss the Margarita Marine Museum. Its exhibit halls show the incredible variety of sea life found along Venezuela's coast.[7]

Sierra Nevada National Park

Deep in the Venezuelan Andes Mountains is Sierra Nevada National Park. Close to Lake Maracaibo, it covers 683,112 acres (276,446 hectares) and contains the highest points of land in the country.[8] Living in that region are condors, spectacled bears, jaguars, red howler monkeys, chestnut eagles, and white-capped parrots. Some of the towering mountain peaks remain covered in snow during summer. There are deep valleys, glaciers, and cold lakes, as well as rushing rivers and streams. People go there to fish, climb, ski, snowboard, hang glide, and mountain bike.

One way to quickly climb a mountain in this park is to take the cable car from the city of Mérida right up to 15,633-foot- (4,765-meter-)

Noisy red howler monkeys live in South and Central American forests. The largest monkeys in the Americas, they usually live in groups of about eighteen.

At more than three miles (five kilometers) above sea level, Bolívar Peak towers over the rest of the Sierra Nevada National Park.

tall Mirror Peak. This is the highest and longest cable car in the world.[9] As you go higher, you can watch as the trees and plants thin out until there are no trees at all. At the top of Mirror Peak, you can see Bolívar Peak, the tallest mountain in Venezuela. It rises 16,437 feet (5,007 meters)—just over 3 miles (5 kilometers) into the sky.

If you happen to visit this park, bring warm clothes even in summer. It gets very cold in those mountains. Also, take it easy the higher you go, because the air up there increasingly lacks oxygen. If you aren't careful, you could get sick or faint.

Lake Maracaibo

An interesting mixture of nature, traditional living, and the modern world coexist at Lake Maracaibo in the state of Zulia. The Guajiro Indians of this region lived there when Columbus arrived. Today, most make their homes in dry land regions and along the coastal areas of Venezuela. Others live in special sections of Zulia's capital city, Maracaibo.[10]

In the days of Columbus, the waters of Lake Maracaibo were clean. You could drink from the lake and swim in it safely. No more. Oilrigs dot the lake and factories crowd its shores. Oil spills, factory waste, and city sewage pollute the lake. Salt water also mixes with the lake water: it enters the lake through a natural canal from the Caribbean Sea. The Venezuelan government continues trying to rid the lake of its pollution and the invasive plant called duckweed. As the pollution-loving duckweed spreads, it blocks sunlight and uses oxygen in the water, which starves and suffocates other organisms living below it.

One awe-inspiring sight in this region is Catatumbo (kah-tah-TOOM-boh) Lightning. This mostly cloud-to-cloud lightning occurs at night where the Catatumbo River empties into Lake Maracaibo. For at least 140 nights a year, you can see an unforgettable all-natural light show.[11]

From the bright city of Caracas to the awesome Angel Falls and the eerie Catatumbo Lightning on Lake Maracaibo, Venezuela offers an inviting mix of beauty and tradition.

Sunset over Lake Maracaibo

Arepas

Arepas (ah-RAY-pahs) look like round flat breads or little pancakes. They are the most common type of food found in Venezuela. People there like them so much that they even have restaurants called *areperas* (ah-RAY-payr-ahs) that serve mostly arepas. It's easy to make them, but please get help from an adult, and wash your hands before you start.

Ingredients
2 cups corn flour
2 teaspoons salt
2 ½ cups warm water
3 tablespoons cooking oil
Butter
Grated cheese or other toppings

Instructions
1. Preheat the oven to 350°F.
2. Put the corn flour in a large bowl.
3. In a measuring cup, mix the salt with the warm water. Slowly add the water to the flour and mix until the flour becomes like a wet paste.
4. Cover the dough and let it sit for about 5 minutes.
5. Wet your hands and make about 8 little balls out of the dough. Then flatten the balls so that they are around 3 inches across and 1 inch thick.
6. Put a frying pan on the stove and pour the oil inside. Turn on the stove to medium heat.
7. Using a spatula, carefully place 3 or 4 arepas into the frying pan. Cook them for about 5 minutes on each side. They should look crusty and brown on both sides. Use the spatula to move the partially cooked arepas to a baking sheet.
8. Repeat step 7 until all the arepas are on the baking sheet. Then bake for 30 minutes.
9. Using oven mitts, take the baking sheet out of the oven. Tap the arepas with the spatula. If they sound hollow, they are done. Remove them from the pan and place them on a plate.
10. When they have cooled slightly, slice open the arepas with a table knife. Top with butter and grated cheese, cooked meat, scrambled eggs, or cooked beans and other vegetables.

Venezuelan

Craft

Devil Dancer Mask

Want a great mask for a costume party or Halloween? Why not create one like the Venezuelan devil dancers wear? There is no one way to make such a mask, so you can't really make a mistake. Besides, it's fun!

Materials
Brown grocery bag (preferably without printing)
Scissors
Glue
Colored markers
Poster board (red, green, yellow, and white—half sheets is all you will need)

Instructions
1. With the help of **an adult**, cut holes in the two narrow sides of the grocery bag so that it will go over your shoulders. Put the bag over your head. Does your head touch the top of the bag? If not, cut both shoulder holes higher until your head does touch.
2. With the bag over your head, reach around in front of you with both hands and touch your eyes. Then have somebody mark a spot where each eye is located. Take the bag off your head and cut out two eyeholes that are big enough for you to see well through.
3. Lay the bag flat. With your markers, draw a great big weird-looking eye around each of the eyeholes.
4. Draw a funny nose between and below the eyes you drew. Make it with two huge circular nostrils. Cut out the nostrils with your scissors so that it will be easy for you to breathe. Draw a huge open mouth below the nose. If you want, make it have an evil smile. Use a black marker and fill in the open mouth completely. Under the mouth, draw a chin and cheeks going up the side of the face.
5. Use markers to draw lips, eyebrows, wrinkles on the forehead, bags under the eyes, and whatever other details you want to add. Fill in the face with wild colors any way you like.
6. Draw these things on different pieces of poster board any color or size you think would look good: ears, horns, tongue, and teeth. Cut out all the pieces with scissors. With the grocery bag lying flat, rest all the pieces on the bag in the right places to see how they look. You might want to cut the bases of the teeth at a slant so that they look like they are behind the lips. If anything looks too big, cut it down. Color them or add detail if you want.
7. Glue on all the pieces: the ears, horns, tongue, and teeth. When the glue is dry, your devil dancer mask will be ready to use.

CHAPTER NOTES

Chapter 1. A Quick Peek
1. Fodor's Travel Publications, Inc., *Fodor's South America* (New York: Fodor's Travel Publications, 2009), p. 730.
2. Ibid., p. 712.
3. Ben Box, *South America Handbook 2009* (Guilford, CT: Globe Pequot Press, 2008), p. 1556.
4. BBC News: Country profile, Venezuela, http://news.bbc.co.uk/2/hi/americas/country_profiles/1229345.stm

Chapter 2. Dipping into the Past
1. Alan Murphy and Mick Day, *Venezuela Handbook* (Bath, England: Footprints Handbooks, 2000), p. 355.
2. Robert Harvey, *Liberators: Latin America's Struggle for Independence* (Woodstock, NY: The Overlook Press, 2000), p. 80.
3. Robert Buckman, *Latin America 2008* (Baltimore: Stryker-Post Publications, 2008), p. 343.
4. Embassy of the Bolívarian Republic of Venezuela in the United States, Culture, History, http://www.embavenez-us.org/index.php?pagina=pag_culture_brief.php&titulo=Culture
5. Michael Reid, *Forgotten Continent: The Battle for Latin America's Soul* (New Haven: Yale University Press, 2007), p. 162.

Chapter 3. Who's in Charge?
1. Michael Reid, *The Battle for Latin America's Soul* (New Haven: Yale University Press, 2007), p. 66.
2. U.S. Department of State: Background Notes, Venezuela, http://www.state.gov/r/pa/ei/bgn/35766.htm
3. Ibid.
4. Ibid.
5. Associated Press, "Venezuela President Hugo Chávez Says Election Gives Him a Mandate," *New York Daily News,* February 16, 2009, http://www.nydailynews.com/news/national/2009/02/16/2009-02-16_venezuela_president_hugo_chavez_says_col.html

Chapter 4. What's Venezuela Really Like?
1. Alan Murphy and Mick Day, *Venezuela Handbook* (Bath, England: Footprints Handbooks, 2000), p. 298.
2. Robert Buckman, *Latin America 2008* (Baltimore: Stryker-Post Publications, 2008), p. 343.
3. Murphy and Day, p. 14.
4. Ibid., p. 368.
5. Bjorn Carey, "Explorers Discover Huge Cave in Venezuela," *MSNBC: Live Science,* February 22, 2006, http://www.msnbc.msn.com/id/11499977
6. National Geographic: Animals, Anaconda, http://animals.nationalgeographic.com/animals/reptiles/green-anaconda.html

Chapter 5. People and Everyday Living
1. U.S. Department of State: Background Notes: Venezuela, http://www.state.gov/r/pa/ei/bgn/35766.htm
2. Fodor's Travel Publications, Inc., *Fodor's South America* (New York: Fodor's Travel Publications, 2009), p. 730.
3. Hands Around the World: Yanomamo Indians, http://indian-cultures.com/Cultures/yanomamo.html
4. Ibid.
5. Library of Congress—Federal Research Division: Country Profile: Venezuela, http://lcweb2.loc.gov/frd/cs/profiles/Venezuela.pdf
6. U.S. Department of State.
7. Mark Dinnen, *Culture and Customs of Venezuela* (Westport, CT: Greenwood Press, 2001), pp. 30–31.
8. Dinnen, pp. 45–46.
9. Ibid., pp. 19–20, 47.
10. Embassy of the Bolívarian Republic of Venezuela in the United States, http://www.embavenez-us.org?pagina=kids.venezuela/education.htm&titulo=venezuelaforkids
11. Alan Murphy and Mick Day, *Venezuela Handbook* (Bath, England: Footprints Handbooks, 2000), p. 83.
12. Dinnen, p. 59.
13. National Geographic: Music, Venezuela, http://worldmusic.nationalgeographic.com/view/page.basic/country/content.country/venezuela_40/en

Chapter 6. Money and Business

1. U.S. Department of State: Background Notes, Venezuela, http://www.state.gov/r/pa/ei/bgn/35766.htm
2. Central Intelligence Agency: *World Factbook*, Venezuela, https://www.cia.gov/library/publications/the-world-factbook/geos/ve.html
3. U.S. Department of State.
4. Ibid.
5. Alan Murphy and Mick Day, *Venezuela Handbook* (Bath, England: Footprints Handbooks, 2000), p. 389.
6. U.S. Department of State.

Chapter 7. Up Close and Personal: Five Stories

1. Christian Red, "Francisco Rodriguez Talks to News From Venezuelan Mountain Top," *New York Daily News*, December 13, 2008, http://www.nydailynews.com/sports/baseball/mets/2008/12/13/2008-12-13_francisco_rodriguez_talks_to_news_from_v.html
2. Cynthia Tompkins and David Foster, *Notable Twentieth-Century Latin American Women* (Westport, CT: Greenwillow Press, 2001), p. 256.
3. BBC World Service, "World, Americas—Beauty Queen Wins State Election," *BBC News*, March 14, 1999, http://news.bbc.co.uk/2/hi/americas/296835.stm
4. Simón Díaz: Biography, http://simondiaz.com/biography.html
5. Carlos A. Solé (ed.), *Latin American Writers*, Vol. 2 (New York: Charles Scribner's Sons, 1989), p. 718.
6. Angel Flores, *Spanish American Authors of the 20th Century* (New York: H. W. Wilson Co., 1992), p. 656.
7. Karen Angel, "The Truth About Jimmie Angel and Angel Falls," *1939 Gran Sabana Expedition*, Jimmie Angel Historical Project, October 2009. http://www.jimmieangel.org/papers1.html

Chapter 8. Holidays and Celebrations

1. Mark Dinnen, *Culture and Customs of Venezuela* (Westport, CT: Greenwood Press, 2001), p. 60.
2. Discover Venezuela: Travel Information, Holidays, http://www.discovervenezuela.com/discovervenezuela/holidays.cfm
3. Dinnen, p. 50.
4. Ibid., p. 52.
5. "Easter Week in Venezuela," *What's on When? Holidays, Venezuela*, http://www.whatsonwhen.com/sisp/index.htm?fx=event&event_id=39032
6. Alan Murphy and Mick Day, *Venezuela Handbook* (Bath, England: Footprints Handbooks, 2000), p. 384.
7. Simon Romero, "Venezuela Dances to Devilish Beat to Promote Tourism," *The New York Times*, June 12, 2007, http://www.nytimes.com/2007/06/12/world/americas/12venez.htm

Chapter 9. We Visit Venezuela

1. Simon Romero, "In Angel Falls, Venezuela, a Forest of Islands," *The New York Times*, January 14, 2007, http://travel.nytimes.com/2007/01/14/travel/14explorer.html
2. Fodor's Travel Publications, Inc., *Fodor's South America* (New York: Fodor's Travel Publications, 2009), p. 762.
3. Ibid.
4. Alan Murphy and Mick Day, *Venezuela Handbook* (Bath, England: Footprints Handbooks, 2000), p. 325.
5. Explore Margarita: The Orinoco Delta, http://www.exploremargarita.com/regions/venezuela_regions_orinocodelta.htm
6. Fodor's Travel Publications, Inc., p. 709.
7. Ibid., 743.
8. "Andes Climbing in Venezuela," *Lost World Adventures*, January 9, 2007, http://www.lostworldadventures.com/activities/climbing/venezuelaclimbing.htm
9. Murphy and Day, p. 189.
10. Ibid., p. 161.
11. Humberto Márquez, "Venezuela, Lightning in the Sky Fed by Underground Methane," *IPS News*, November 17, 2007, http://ipsnews.net/news.asp?idnews=40101

1498	Christopher Columbus explores Venezuela; he calls the people who live there Indians. He claims the area for Spain.
1525	The first Africans are brought to Venezuela as slaves.
1567	Caracas is founded.
1777	Spain begins to increase control of Venezuela, causing problems with the colonists and the native people.
1811	On July 5, Francisco de Miranda declares Venezuela free from Spain and the War for Independence begins.
1813	Simón Bolívar begins his crusade to free Venezuela and other parts of Latin America from Spain.
1821	Bolívar and his soldiers defeat the Spanish, freeing the present-day countries of Venezuela, Colombia, Panama, and Ecuador. Together, those places are named the Republic of Gran Colombia; Bolívar becomes its president.
1830	The Republic of Gran Colombia falls apart. Venezuela becomes an independent country, with José Antonio Páez as its first president. Bolívar dies.
1854	The slaves are freed.
1859	The Federal War to determine which group will control Venezuela begins. It will last four years.
1902	European countries use ships to blockade Venezuelan ocean trade in an effort to collect Venezuela's debts.
1908	Juan Vicente Gómez becomes dictator of Venezuela; he will stay in power until 1935.
1922	Vast amounts of oil are discovered in the Lake Maracaibo region. Venezuela soon becomes an oil exporting country.
1958	Romulo Betancourt, Venezuela's first democratically elected leader, becomes president.
1976	The Venezuelan government takes over the country's oil industry.
1989	People riot in Caracas over economic problems. Many are killed or injured.
1992	Military officers, including Hugo Chávez, twice try to take over the government and fail.
1999	Hugo Chávez becomes president and establishes a new constitution.
2002	The people riot against Chávez, who is arrested and then freed by the military.
2006	Hugo Chávez is reelected president.
2008	China builds and puts in space a communications satellite for Venezuela.
2009	Voters allow Hugo Chávez to run for president as many times as he wants.
2010	Chávez sends oil experts to Cuba in order to help that country protect itself against a huge oil spill near Louisiana in the Gulf of Mexico.

FURTHER READING

Books

Hernandez, Rodger. *South America: Facts & Figures*. Broomall, PA: Mason Crest, 2009.
Jones, Helga. *Venezuela*. Minneapolis: Lerner Publications Group, 2008.
Kohen, Jane. *Venezuela*. Tarrytown, NY: Marshall Cavendish, 2002.
Pohl, Kathleen. *Looking at Venezuela*. New York: Gareth Stevens, 2008.
Shields, Charles. *Venezuela*. Broomall, PA: Mason Crest, 2008.

Works Consulted

"Andes Climbing in Venezuela." *Lost World Adventures,* January 9, 2007. http://www.
    lostworldadventures.com/activities/climbing/venezuelaclimbing.htm
Angel, Karen. "The Truth About Jimmie Angel and Angel Falls." 1939 Gran Sabana Expedition.
    Jimmie Angel Historical Project, October 2009. http://www.jimmieangel.org/papers1.html
Associated Press. "Venezuela President Hugo Chávez Says Election Gives Him a Mandate."
    New York Daily News, February 16, 2009. http://www.nydailynews.com/news/us_
    world/2009/02/16/2009-02-16_venezuela_president_hugo_Chávez_says_col.html
BBC News: Country profile, Venezuela. http://news.bbc.co.uk/2/hi/americas/country_
    profiles/1229345.stm
BBC World Service. "World, Americas—Beauty Queen Wins State Election." *BBC News,*
    March 14, 1999, http://news.bbc.co.uk/2/hi/americas/296835.stm
Box, Ben. *South America Handbook 2009*. Guilford, CT: Globe Pequot Press, 2008.

Buckman, Robert. *Latin America 2008.* Baltimore: Stryker-Post Publications, 2008.

Carey, Bjorn. "Explorers Discover Huge Cave in Venezuela." *MSNBC: Live Science,* February 22, 2006. http://www.msnbc.msn.com/id/11499977

Central Intelligence Agency: World Factbook—Venezuela. https://www.cia.gov/library/publications/the-world-factbook/geos/ve.html

Díaz, Simón: Biography, http://simondiaz.com/biography.html

Dinnen, Mark. *Culture and Customs of Venezuela.* Westport, CT: Greenwood Press, 2001.

Discover Venezuela: Travel Information, Holidays. http://www.discovervenezuela.com/discovervenezuela/holidays.cfm

"Easter Week in Venezuela." What's on When? Holidays, Venezuela, http://www.whatsonwhen.com/sisp/index.htm?fx=event&event_id=39032

Embassy of the Bolívarian Republic of Venezuela in the United States, Culture, History. http://www.embavenez-us.org/index.php?pagina=pag_culture_brief.php&titulo=Culture

Explore Margarita: The Orinoco Delta, http://www.exploremargarita.com/regions/venezuela_regions_orinocodelta.htm

Flores, Angel. *Spanish American Authors of the 20th Century.* New York: H.W. Wilson Co., 1992.

Fodor's Travel Publications, Inc. *Fodor's South America.* New York: Fodor's Travel Publications, 2009.

Hands Around the World: Yanomamo Indians, http://indian-cultures.com/Cultures/yanomamo.html

Harvey, Robert. *Liberators: Latin America's Struggle for Independence.* Woodstock, New York: The Overlook Press, 2000.

Library of Congress—Federal Research Division: Country Profile: Venezuela, http://lcweb2.loc.gov/frd/cs/vetoc.html

Marcano, Christina, and Alberto Tyszka. *Hugo Chávez.* New York: Random House, 2006.

Márquez, Humberto. "Venezuela, Lightning in the Sky Fed by Underground Methane." *IPS News,* November 17, 2007, http://ipsnews.net/news.asp?idnews=40101

Murphy, Alan, and Mick Day. *Venezuela Handbook.* Bath, England: Footprints Handbooks, 2000.

National Geographic: Animals, Anaconda, http://animals.nationalgeographic.com/animals/reptiles/green-anaconda.html

National Geographic: Music, Venezuela, http://worldmusic.nationalgeographic.com/view/page.basic/country/content.country/venezuela_40/en

Red, Christian. "Francisco Rodriguez Talks to News From Venezuelan Mountain Top." *New York Daily News,* December 13, 2008. http://www.nydailynews.com/sports/baseball/mets/2008/12/13/2008-12-13_francisco_rodriguez_talks_to_news_from_v.html

Reid, Michael. *Forgotten Continent: The Battle for Latin America's Soul.* New Haven, CT: Yale University Press, 2007.

Romero, Simon. "In Angel Falls, Venezuela, a Forest of Islands." *The New York Times,* January 14, 2007. http://travel.nytimes.com/2007/01/14/travel/14explorer.html

———. "Venezuela Dances to Devilish Beat to Promote Tourism." *The New York Times,* June 12, 2007. http://www.nytimes.com/2007/06/12/world/americas/12venez.htm

Solé, Carlos A. (ed.). *Latin American Writers (Vol. 2).* New York: Charles Scribner's Sons, 1989.

Tompkins, Cynthia, and David Foster. *Notable Twentieth-Century Latin American Women.* Westport, CT: Greenwillow Press, 2001.

U.S. Department of State: Background Notes, Venezuela, http://www.state.gov/r/pa/ei/bgn/35766.htm

On the Internet

Embassy of the Bolívarian Republic of Venezuela in the United States, Venezuela for Kids http://lcweb2.loc.gov/frd/cs/profiles/Venezuela.pdf

National Geographic: The Orinoco http://video.nationalgeographic.com/video/player/places/parks-and-nature-places/lakes-and-rivers/venezuela_orinoco.html

Venezuelan Analysis: News, Views, and Analysis http://venezuelanalysis.com/

Virtual Andean Tourist Routes: Sierra Nevada National Park http://www.comunidadandina.org/ingles/tourism/parks/i_sierra.htm

archipelago (ar-kih-PEH-leh-goh)—A chain of islands.

arepa (ah-RAY-pah)—A fried or baked corn cake.

bauxite (BAWK-syt)—The ore from which aluminum is extracted.

cacao (kuh-KAY-oh)—A plant whose seeds are used to make chocolate.

capybara (kap-uh-BAYR-uh) A very large water-loving mammal that is related to the guinea pig.

chevre (CHEH-veh-reh)—"Cool," or very okay.

civil war—War between people of the same country.

comptroller (KOM-troh-ler)—Someone who keeps track of the finances in a business or government.

cuatro (KWAH-troh)—A Venezuelan four-stringed guitar.

delta—A triangle of mud formed where a river empties into a larger body of water.

federal republic—A country in which people elect a national government as well as governments for each of its states.

indigenous (in-DIJ-uh-ness)—Something or someone that is native to a certain location.

inflation (in-FLAY-shun)—The rising cost of goods when money loses some of its value.

joropo (hoh-ROH-poh)—Venezuela's national dance from Los Llanos.

Los Llanos (LOHS YAH-nohs)—The flatlands of Venezuela.

llaneros (yah-NAYR-rohs)—The cowboys of Los Llanos.

ombudsman (OM-budz-mun)—A government official who investigates complaints (such as by consumers against a company) and tries to resolve them.

pabellón criollo (pay-bel-YOHN KREE-yoh)—Venezuela's national dish, it is a combination of shredded beef, rice, fried plantains, yucca, black beans, and grated cheese.

peninsula (puh-NIN-soo-lah)—A strip of land surrounded by water on three sides.

piranhas (pih-RON-uhs)—Small flesh-eating fish with big teeth.

plantain (plan-TAYN)—A tropical plant with banana-like fruit.

sorghum (SOR-gum)—A type of grain.

souvenir (soo-veh-NEER)—An item people keep to remind them of an event or a person.

tepui (tey-POO-ee)—A flat-topped mountain.

textiles—Cloth products.

tuberculosis (too-bur-kyuh-LOH-sihs)—A dangerous disease of the lungs.

yucca (YUK-ah)—A plant with sword-shaped leaves and white flowers.

PHOTO CREDITS: Cover, pp. 1, 2–3, 8, 25, 26, 38, 40, 41, 42, 48, 54—cc-by-sa-2.0; pp. 10–11, 47, 52, 53—cc-by-nc-nd-sa-2.0; p. 16—Arturo Michelena; p. 17—John Dominis/Time & Life Pictures/Getty Images; pp. 18, 21—Jorge Silva/Reuters/Corbis; pp. 20, 28—cc-by-sa-2.5; pp. 22, 46, 51, 55—cc-by-nc-sa-2.0; p. 27—Z. Leszczynski/Animals Animals; p. 31—AP Photo/Leslie Mazoch; p. 34—Gabriel Rivera/Corbis; p. 37—cc-by-sa-3.0; p. 57—Doug Dillon; p. 64—Greg Dillon. Every effort has been made to locate all copyright holders of material used in this book. If any errors or omissions have occurred, corrections will be made in future editions of the book.

Africa, Africans   30, 32, 33, 47
Amazonas   12, 29
Andes   24, 26, 53
Angel, Jimmie   31, 39, 42, 43, 50
Angel Falls   39, 42, 43, 50
Atlantic Ocean   12, 23
baseball   32, 38, 39
beauty contests/queens   32, 40
Betancourt, Romulo   17
Bolívar, Simón   15, 16, 17, 19, 43, 49
Bolívar Fuerte (Strong Bolívar)   13, 37
Bolívar Peak   13, 54
Brazil   6, 7, 10, 12, 32
bullfights   9
Caracas   10–11, 12, 13, 20, 24, 30, 31,
    33, 38, 39, 40, 46, 47, 49–50
Caribbean Sea   6, 7, 10, 12, 13, 22, 24,
    31, 39, 40, 44, 46, 47, 49
Carnival   46
Catatumbo (lightning)   55
Central America   7, 37
Chávez, Hugo   13, 17, 19, 20, 21, 37, 40
chevre   9
Colombia   6, 7, 12, 15, 21, 23, 30, 32
Columbus, Christopher   9, 15, 55
constitution   19, 20, 21
coral reefs   22, 23, 24
Corpus Christi   47
cowboys   16, 25
Cuba   6, 7
Dancing Devils   47, 48
Delta Amacuro   12, 50
Díaz, Simón   39, 40–41, 46
Europe, European   12, 24, 30, 32, 37
Gómez, Juan Vicente   16
Gran Colombia, Republic of   16
Guyana   7, 12, 25
Holy Week   45, 47
Houses of the Gods   25
Innocents, Day of   46
Latin America   6, 7, 16, 32, 35, 47, 48
Los Llanos   25, 26, 33, 40
Los Roques   22, 23
Machado, Antonio   31–32
Maracaibo, Lake   12, 24, 30, 53, 55
Margarita Island   12, 23, 51, 52
Michelena, Arturo   16
Mirror Peak   54
Mount Roraima   25
North America   7
oil   13, 19, 24, 26, 34, 35, 55
Orinoco Delta   50
Orinoco River   23
pabellón criollo   33
Parra, Teresa de la   39, 41, 43

Portuguese   6
Rodriguez, Francisco (K-Rod)   38, 39
Sáez, Irene   19, 39, 40, 46
South America   6, 7, 9, 15, 23, 24, 29, 53
Spain, Spanish   6, 9, 13, 15, 16, 30, 32,
    34, 43, 46, 55
telenovelas   32
tepuis   9, 25, 26, 42, 43, 56
Trinidad and Tobago   12, 23
United Nations   18, 32, 46
United States   6, 17, 29, 32
Venezuela
    cities of   11, 12, 13, 23, 29, 43, 55
    climate of   10, 13, 27, 54
    deserts in   26, 27
    economy and finances of   11, 13, 16, 19,
        24, 29, 34–37
    family and women in   30, 31
    famous people of   15, 16, 17, 18, 19, 20,
        21, 39–43
    farming and agriculture in   4, 37
    flatlands in   4, 25
    food and drink in   30, 33, 37, 45, 51, 56
    geography of   9, 10, 12, 13, 22–27, 50,
        51
    government and politics in   9, 13, 19–21,
        23, 35, 37, 40
    highlands and mountains in   9, 23, 25,
        42, 43, 54
    history of   8, 9, 14, 15–17, 37, 45 47,
        48, 49
    holidays, festivals, and celebrations in
        8, 9, 44, 45–47
    Indians in   9, 14, 15, 25, 28, 29, 30, 33,
        50, 51, 55
    literacy in   13, 31
    map of   12
    music, dance, and performing arts in   8,
        25, 32, 33, 40, 41, 45
    national parks in   10, 33, 50, 54, 55
    natural resources of   13, 17, 19, 34, 35
    people, culture, and lifestyles in   8, 9,
        11, 13, 21, 28–33, 41, 45, 50, 55, 57
    ports of   24, 37
    religion in   9, 13, 30, 45, 46, 47
    rivers and deltas in   23, 25, 27, 29, 35,
        36, 50
    schools in   31, 35
    sea coast and islands of   22, 23, 24, 33,
        37, 50, 51, 52
    sports and recreation in   23, 24, 32, 33,
        52
    universities   31, 41
    wildlife in   13, 23, 24, 25, 26, 27, 29,
        49, 50, 51, 53

Doug Dillon lives with his wife, Barbara, in Florida, where he writes for young people and adults. For many years, he taught geography and history in grades seven to twelve. Two states, Michigan and Washington, use some of his articles published in *Boy's Life* magazine for their statewide student testing programs.

Doug Dillon is a full member of the Society of Children's Book Writers and Illustrators. His books include *A Brief Political and Geographic History of Asia* and *Class Trip: St. Augustine* for Mitchell Lane Publishers.